THE SOLE JOURNEY OF SOUL

JAS TAYLOR

Printed in United Sates
ISBN: 978-0-578-93691-8

Jas Taylor

Book II.

Contents

Signs

There is always a sign.
There is always a change.
Subtle changes.
A change in pace of the wind,
A change in the way leaves softly plummet
To be cradled by the ground of the earth.
The sky blackens as cumulus clouds hover
Over the atmosphere.
A peculiar scent lingers.
A whiff of the crisp, soothing air;
My nostrils are acquainted with the aroma.
There is always a sign before the storm.
There is always a change.
If I am cognizant, are the signs still subtle?

Solitude

How comfortable are you with me?
Do you embrace me or do you run?
Do you search for my presence or is it shunned?
How cherished am I to you?
I come in peace to help you on your journey.
I am certain you will appreciate and thank me
But I must warn you;
Take heed.
I will pull you to a depth you cannot fathom.
I am selfish and require your attention.
I crave aloneness with you.
Your stillness is familiar to me.
In your seclusion, there you will find me.
I abide in your silence with contentment.
I will peel you away layer by layer to learn you.
I will strip you with gratitude.
I will expose you with a sly grin.
Feebleness cannot reside here but all in good reason.
Do you trust me?

Grounded

Balance.
Life requires balance.
Crops must be watered for growth
But a seed must be planted first.
A seed cannot develop
Without the soil of the earth.
The sprout cannot exist
Without being submerged by rain.
It cannot grow roots without being
Anchored into the ground.
The ground produces life.
It is the bridge between seed and harvest.
It is the gatekeeper of nourishment.
We are made from it and shall one day return.
It is the beginning and end of the cycle.
Find comfort here;
It’s essential for growth.

Sideline

The urge to be seen,
The urge to be heard.
The urge to be loved,
The urge to be served.
The urge to be influential,
The urge to be praised.
The urge to be known
But is it all in vain?
The urge to be the star,
The urge to always impress.
The urge is strong and tempting
But the background carries the test.
Every phase in life has purpose
I'll welcome each one with my best.
I pray to embrace the sideline,
There I shall find clarity and rest.

Looking Glass

When faced with my image, who do I really see?
Do I see the work of God or do I just see me?
Do I nitpick any flaws or do I focus on God's face?
Do I become conceited?
Or instead reflect on His grace?
Do I thank God for this temple?
Or do I criticize what I want to change?
Do I embrace the person He made me?
Or in the mirror can I only see pain?
Do I ignore my character shortcomings?
Do I accept them, learn and grow?
Do I really believe I have purpose?
Or only because some told me so?
Do I want to change for the better?
Am I willing to put in the work?
Do I really trust in God?
Do I believe He loved me first?
Life is not always clear
But God's grace shall remain true.
I shall strip myself until you are left
To be a direct reflection of you.

Soul Deep

Beauty is skin deep.
A concept pushed by a society
That is image-driven.
It's a contradiction, really.
Physical beauty is overrated
Yet we kill ourselves to reach
An unrealistic image ingrained into
Our conscience from adolescence.
Outer beauty is surface level.
We've read similar words casually flipping
Through the crisp pages of magazines
While subsequent articles address image distortion.
We covet perfection.
We move the post to unachievable goals.
We are walking paradoxes
Plagued by insecurities.
We chase the high of a potentially perfected persona.
Greed.
Envy.
Discontentment.
At what point does one reach satisfaction?
At what point is one content?
Physical beauty is fleeting.

Do we really resonate with that?
Or do we embrace that statement in the moment
To prove we're more than one dimensional?
Beauty is in the eye of the beholder.
One's personal gaze uniquely defines beauty.
How does one view it?
How does one define it?
What does one believe constitutes beauty?
Is it only the shape of one's eyes?
Or the gentleness that resides in them?
Is it just the curve of one's physique?
Or the meek spirit it houses?
Is it the attraction to one's lips?
Or the encouraging words uttered from them?
The shade of one's complexion?
Or how well they treat the person
Whose skin is different?
Are we solely motivated by personal gain?
Or out of a pure love for others?
If physical beauty is skin deep,
How deep should the beauty of one's soul go?

Inspired by: I Samuel 16:7
Matthew 23:25-28

Riverbend

Life on the straight and narrow gets complicated
When the path gets eroded from life.
It becomes more difficult maneuvering through
The twists and turns.
Never knowing what awaits at the turn of a corner.
Never knowing what's on the other side
At the bend of a road.
It's not an easy journey,
But I guess it was never meant to be, right?

Seasons

Like nature, one's personal life has seasons.
A season of growth, a season of change.
A season of celebration and others that bring rain.
Each season lays groundwork for the next.
The spring rain prepares the ground for
New flowers to blossom.
Winter sheds away the old to make room for new.
Each season is unique yet seamlessly works together.
Though some seasons are more favored,
Each is necessary to keep and
Maintain nature's balance.
No matter the current season in one's life,
Stay prepared and ready.
After all, harsh conditions don't last forever.

April Showers

Dreary days, overcast grays.
Life seems to emulate April's rain.
Cool brisk nights and darkened skies,
Mundane routines, barely getting by.
Things aren't perfect but I dare not mope
For God's rain replenishes, brings growth and hope.
Hope for warmth and sunnier days.
Hope for new blooms like a Saturday in May.
I splash in the puddle of my tears.
The bass of thunder makes me dance.
It may be pouring now
But it produces life when given the chance.

Wade in the Water

As I stride in the deep
I look to you to trouble life's waters with healing.
I sit in the shadows, waiting
For your signal to lead me.
You shall lead me to my land of Canaan.
My shepherd.
I shall follow you across the river
To the land of milk and honey.
I am battered, torn, escaping life's shackles
Trying to reach freedom in you.
Guide me to my promise land.
Help me carry on.
I'll cross life's murky waters to experience your glory
This side of heaven.
I'll be met by freedom's sweet face
On the other side.
I shall not fear what waits for me in this life.
God's gon' trouble life's waters.

Seek Ye First

Nightfall seems to grow longer.

Light is dwindling.

It's getting tougher to see.

Lord, please guide me through this life journey.

The Unknown

I wander this dim road, wondering
When will I reach you?
Your guidebook beams to illuminate my path.
But these dark roads. . .
Adversity and suffering won't succeed but
You never said it wouldn't form.
I keep hearing something.
Something is lurking in the shadows and
I'm afraid to turn around.
It keeps trying to follow me but
Every time I raise the lamp you gave me,
It seems to go away.
Well whatever it is seems to not like light.
I'm conflicted.
I'm scared but you told me I shouldn't be.
I've never liked change and this road looks different.
I keep trying to read this guidebook to recognize
Signs but I keep getting distracted.
I know something is following me.
This guidebook is telling me to go one way
But my mind is telling me to go another.
Am I going the right way?
This sign looks familiar, did I already pass this?

Maybe I should just turn around.
The echo of my thoughts is too loud.
Are you sure this is the right path?
I don't see anyone.
This can't be right.
This guidebook keeps saying this is the
Direction I'm supposed to go.
My mind keeps racing I can't focus on the signs
Your guide instructs me to follow.
It's still following me.
Whatever it is, is still following me.
I'm trying to focus on this road to get to you.
I raise the lamp you gave me to see but whatever is
Trying to follow me went away again.
It's making me paranoid.
This is the right way, right?
Am I going the right way?

Outcry

I drift, paddling through a sea of overwhelming
Thoughts and hardships that are trying to drown me.
I am wading in depths I can't swim in.
My aggravated shriek could shake
The gates of heaven.
Was this the plan?

Let You Love Me

Scars that go deeper than skin.
Pain only your medicinal hand can heal.
Brokenness only you can mend.
Wholesome peace that only you reveal.
A compulsive over thinker, overrun by fear.
A lethal past you use to produce life.
A tiny, anguished being you long to be near.
A sensitive soul you value above a man-made price.
The rose made of concrete.
The mortal burned in the fire and birthed
From the ashes.
A clueless creature you work overtime to comfort.
I am a product of survival.
And yet, you wait with open arms.
You immerse me in a love
Deep enough to heal the wounds of past generations.
Your grace shall runneth over.
Your compassion shall runneth over.
Your love shall runneth over into my heart
Until it is made whole.

Waves

Nothing in this life seems to stay consistent.
Why don't the pleasant thoughts last?
My emotions are ever-changing.
The flashbacks continue to haunt me.
The sadness comes in waves.
It's as dynamic as the strength of tides.
It rocks me to and fro.
Be my anchor through life's storms.
Hold me steady through the seas of depression.
Ground me through the ups and downs.
Be the constant in the midst of life's inconsistencies.
Through life's choppiness, keep me tied to you.

Shadow Man

It's a never-ending tug-of-war game with you.
My mind has been held captive by its own hands as it fights for freedom from itself.
The fight against myself to seek freedom in God continues.
I lurk in the shadows, anticipating my own downfall.
My mind seethes at the thought of overcoming itself.
I am my worst enemy and biggest threat.
My adversary.
The toughest battles are spiritual.
The daily battle against myself continues on but I do not fret.
I shall prepare for combat against my reflection.
Some battles along this journey may be lost but I rest in the truth.
Every fight may not be in my favor but I shall win the war.

Overflow

God,

I ask that your Spirit overtakes me.

Drown me in your presence.

Allow your love to be so enticing it suffocates all doubt and anxiety.

Let my spirit swell from the overabundance of your presence.

Overtake me until your grace touches every soul connected to mine.

Let your love downpour in my heart until it spills into every facet of my life.

Fill me until my seams burst from your infectious joy.

Cradle my mind in your hands until it is renewed.

Be housed in my temple.

Flood my heart with your love until the pain is washed away.

Let your Spirit be so overwhelming I am unrecognizable through fleshly eyes.

Fill me.

Pour into me.

Overtake me.

Let my being be submerged in you.

Through the Fire

God has not given me the spirit of fear.
I will fight every battle until I come out on the other side.
Never shall I be afraid.
Though I walk through the darkest valleys, I will fear no evil.
I will fear no test.
I will fear no stronghold.
I will not fear death.
God comforts me on this journey to freedom in Him.
You have overcome this life and victory shall continue with me.
My adversary shall watch me dance in the fire it threw me in.
It will know my name.
The Word, like a baton, was handed off to my generation.
We will rise.
We shall take every stone shucked to create shields for war.
Every battle scar will be a testament of your given strength and ability to help us overcome.
Every spiritual giant shall be slain.

We are a force to be reckoned with.
We are not here to appease.
We are not here to conform.
We are here to shake tables.
We are here to challenge.
We plan and prepare.
We shall not succumb to our spiritual warfare.
We shall not succumb to our minds.
We shall not succumb to distractions.
Your Word shall guide us.
Your Spirit shall encourage us.
Your grace shall cover us.
Your mercy shall empower us.
May God bless us on this journey.

Inspired by the story of Shadrach,
Meshach & Abednego (Daniel chapter 3)

Jas Taylor always found comfort through pen and paper. As Taylor spent hours filling spirals, diaries and memo pads with fictional tales, poems and thoughts, the imaginative, inner world became a safe haven and continues to serve as a therapeutic form of self-expression. Graduating from Missouri Western State University in 2017, Taylor studied journalism at the institution and published her first fiction piece through an online writing contest.

Other work by Taylor include the poetry book *A Psalm Unto You* and lifestyle blog *Modest Petals* found at the website handle www.modestpetals.com. Taylor also plans to release a children's book and prayerfully, a few novels in the near future.

The following pages are entirely for you. Feel free to journal, write down prayers, thoughts, use it as a space to house your doodles or even your own poems. Use the pages as you see fit.

Thank you so much for taking the time to read the words on the previous pages.

Psalm 116:16-17

Jas Taylor

Daniel 4:1-3

Romans 10:8-9

Romans 8:28

Isaiah 55:6

Proverbs 3:25-26

www.ingramcontent.com/pod-product-compliance
Lightning Source LLC
Chambersburg PA
CBHW020448030426
42337CB00014B/1451
9780578936918